an eventful display

Patricia Harrison

The children in Wavendon Gate Combined School, Milton Keynes, produced all of the displays in this book. Of course they did get a little help from their teachers and other adults who work in the classrooms!

The author and publisher would like to thank the following individuals for their invaluable support during the preparation of this book.

Alison Goodman

Amanda Dewhirst

Andrea Russell

Catherine O'Connell

Gretta Funnell

Heather Goddard

Jane Kozykowska

Joanne Brown

Judith Alexander

Kirk Hopkins

Linzi Clegg

Lizzie Viner

Pauline Allonby

Trevor Wilkinson

Victoria Wallis

Vida Peters

Wendy Marfleet

A special thanks goes to Noel McHugh and Linda Killman who coordinated the work in the school.

Sunflowers display from page 32

First published in 2003 by BELAIR PUBLICATIONS LIMITED
Apex Business Centre, Boscombe Road, Dunstable, Beds LU5 4RL
© 2003 Folens on behalf of the author Patricia Harrison
Reprinted 2004.

Freelance Publisher and Designer: Patricia Harrison
Design and page layout: Ed Gallagher   **Cover Design:** Duncan McTeer
Photography: Steve Harrison p5 (right), page 28 (bottom), page 30.
All other photographs by Kelvin Freeman

The Lord of the Rings by J.R.R. Tolkien (HarperCollins, 1954) Copyright © J.R.R. Tolkien, 1954. Characters from *The Lord of the Rings* used by permission of HarperCollins on behalf of The Tolkien Estate.

ISBN 0 94788 299 5

Introduction

Display is so vital for a number of reasons. It helps create the 'first impression' that is so important in projecting the values of the school to parents, the local community, and to all visitors.

Display also speaks volumes about the value the school places on the learning environment children deserve and the importance that is placed on the work children produce.

Children encouraged to produce their best written and artistic work deserve nothing less than having that high quality work displayed to the highest standard. It helps reinforce a sense of pride and higher self-esteem, and it also indicates that the school is not just paying lip-service to the mantra of 'do your best', but reflecting its words in its practice.

This book highlights display opportunities and techniques all around the school - from the entrance, through corridors and into the classroom. It seeks to exemplify work from across the curriculum in displays and to explore opportunities for motivating pupils through display-focused activities. The educational rationale behind the display, the materials and techniques used and the approach adopted are recurring features of the double page spreads.

I hope there is something here for all teachers and that your school will benefit from at least some of the ideas contained within these pages.

Patricia Harrison

When I Look Up

Some classrooms lack available wall space, others have very high ceilings. Using the space above our heads can be very effective.

washing line

Washing lines are a great idea. They can be a permanent feature of any classroom and can be used to display work in most curriculum areas. The number lines on this page hang in an early years classroom but the numbers used can reflect work with any age group.

Warning

Hanging displays can set off alarms. Check out the location of sensors before hanging anything.

Other ideas

- History – timeline
- Geography – routes
- Design – sequence
- Literacy – prompt sheets
- Science – recording an investigation

YOU WILL NEED

- strong string
- spring pegs

0.1 0.2 0.3 0.4 0.5 0

snake number line

The snake was originally created when the children (aged 7) were studying the Chinese New Year. The design linked to the children's artwork and is in the style of Clarice Cliff. The mathematics co-ordinator saw an opportunity to give the snake a longer life!

September

YOU WILL NEED

- paper plates
- split pins
- felt tips
- string
- numbers
- large card

approach

- Each child has a paper plate, draws out sections and colours them using bright coloured felt pens. Each section is outlined in black.

- Link all the plates together using split pins to form the body.

- Make a head and tail from card and staple to each end of the body.

- Use string to hang and then suspend numbers or words from each plate.

MONET 1ST

EMILY 5TH

Phillippa 17

SEBASTIAN 18TH

Nathaniel 22

CIARON 24TH

RYAN 25TH

10 20 30 40 50 60 70 80 90

0.7 **0.8** **0.9**

months timeline

The timeline shown here is used to teach young children the months of the year and is linked to the children's birthdays. All 12 months are displayed. The idea could be used to depict events e.g. festivals.

October

November

December

seascape

The display is linked to the children's work (aged 4-5) on patterns and colour.

approach

- Attach material to a table. Use boxes underneath to create different levels.

- Thread green raffia through the netting.

- Create fish using card fish outlines. Cover with rainbow tissue and paint with diluted PVA. Decorate with sequins.

- Create the sea using blue and green cellophane and mix with silver, thin ribbon.

YOU WILL NEED

- coloured cellophane
- silver ribbon
- sequins
- paint
- shells
- pva (watered down)
- raffia
- netting
- rainbow tissue
- thread
- small boxes
- card

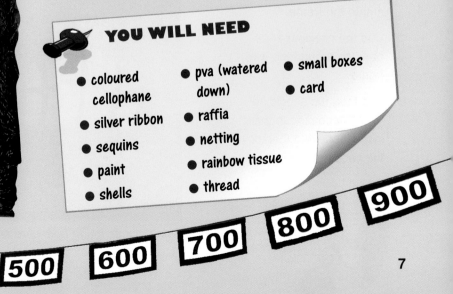

200 300 400 500 600 700 800 900

MOBILES

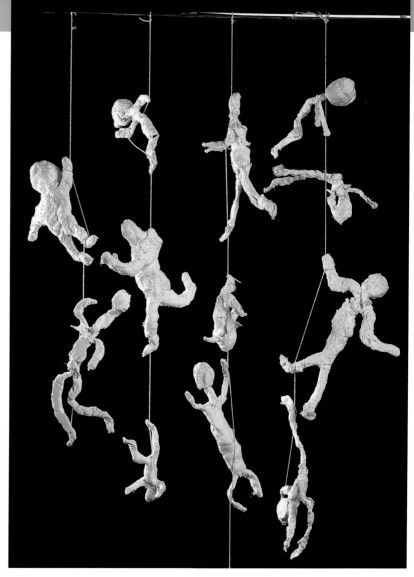

people in action

The Mod roc figures were created as part of the children's' work (aged 11) on the topic 'People in Action'. Children explored dynamic activities such as dance, gymnastics and sport and also examined the proportion of body parts.

YOU WILL NEED

- modelling wire
- newspaper
- Mod roc

approach

- Use the modelling wire to create the frame.

- Use the newspaper as padding around the wire frame.

- The Mod roc should be mixed according to the instructions and then cover the padding with it.

Ships mobile made from card and modelling wire

carousel books

The children (aged 9) looked at books that have pictures that give additional information to the text. The idea for making the carousel books came from *'Making Books' by Paul Jackson published by A & C Black.*

ideas for using carousel books

Carousel books can be used in different curriculum areas. There are four openings. The carousel books in the photograph were produced as part of a study of animals. Some children chose four different animals, others chose to draw and write about four features of the same animal. Other ideas might include four rooms in a house, four seasons, different weather conditions, four stages of growing up, caterpillar to butterfly – four stages of development etc.

YOU WILL NEED

- A3 paper
- scissors
- glue
- colouring material
- small paper clips
- string

9

Books Books Books

mix 'n' match

'Mix 'n' match' is an interactive activity that can be used with most books. It will improve children's observation skills and their ability to write character descriptions. *The stimulus for this display was The Lord of the Rings by JRR Tolkien, published by Harper Collins.*

approach

- Children choose a character from the book. They draw or paint the character based on the description in the book. They do not label their drawing.

- On a separate piece of paper they write a character description.

  - Pictures and descriptions are laminated.

  - The pictures and descriptions are mixed up and attached to the wall display with Velcro.

- Individually or in pairs children can read the descriptions and move them on the display so they match the picture of the character they describe,

large images

- The characters on these pages were drawn by two very talented 10 year olds at full size. They painted what they felt a wizard would look like.

- If your children would have difficulty drawing such large-scale pictures they can produce a small drawing, trace onto an OHT and then project onto a wall.

YOU WILL NEED

- paint
- paper
- backing paper
- velcro
- laminate
- card

LORD *of the* RINGS

MIX 'N' MATCH

Can you match the character to the correct name and description?

Gimli

Bilbo

Galadriel

Saruman

Gandalf

Arwen

Bywater   Hobbiton
Brandywine River   Bag End

We used ICT to design the lettering on the signpost. We also used it for word processing our book reviews.

YOU WILL NEED

- labels
- computer
- broom
- paint

approach

- The signpost and labels were produced using Microsoft® Publisher.®

It was rumoured that the Dark Tower had been rebuilt.

The Dark Tower of Mordor

The Hobbits knew about the Dark Tower as a legend from the distant past.

In Art we painted the Dark Tower.

Terrible creatur were thought to live in the Dark Tower.

approach

- Children use ICT to create lists, descriptions, book reviews and character descriptions.

- Ideally the book covers should be designed at the end of the topic so that children can make a considered decision as to what cover would be most appropriate.

We designed book covers

BOOK REVIEW
Lord of the Rings by JRR Tolkien

The author is JRR Tolkien. The publisher is Harper Collins. It was first published in 1954. The story is about a Hobbit called Frodo who tries to protect the ring which is all powerful and if it gets into the wrong hands it would mean evil would spread all over the world.

There are lots of main characters,these include the five Hobbits: Bilbo, Frodo,, Merry, Pippin and Sam. Characters who are not Hobbits are Gandalf, Saruman, Celeborn, Galadriel, Legolas, Elrond, Arwen, Gimli, Aragorn and Boromir.
My favourite character is Frodo because he is daring and adventurous.

My favourite bit in the book is when the Hobbits were being chased by the dark rider on horseback. I think the story is FANTASTIC!

"Little pig, little pig, let me come in."

The Three Little Pigs

"...No...No...No... not by the hair of my chinny chin chin. I will not let you in"

Once upon a time

The first little pig built his house out of straw

The second little pig built her house out of sticks.

third little pig built his house out of bricks.

"Then I'll Huff, and I'll Puff, and I'll blow your house down"

approach

- The pigs and house were drawn and cut out by an adult.

- Create a textured effect on the pigs by using a mixture of paint and sand.

- Use tracing paper to create patterns for the clothes. Children can trace the outline of the clothes, cut them out, and make clothes out of wallpaper, material and lace.

- The children can decorate the pigs with sequins.

- Use spaghetti for the 'straw' house and glaze with a PVA and water mix.

- Use art straws for the 'stick' house, then paint and glaze.

- Corrugated card rectangles can be used for the 'brick' house.

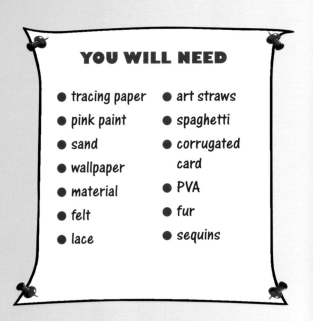

YOU WILL NEED

- tracing paper
- pink paint
- sand
- wallpaper
- material
- felt
- lace
- art straws
- spaghetti
- corrugated card
- PVA
- fur
- sequins

14

The Little Red Hen

The theme for the topic with 5 year olds was '*Do be helpful*'. The stimulus used was the traditional tale '*The Little Red Hen*'.

approach

- Hen and bread: tape scrunched-up newspaper to cut-out shapes of bread and hen.
- Dip the kitchen roll in PVA + water (3:1) and cover the shapes. Use several layers.
- Put in a warm cupboard to dry over the weekend.
- Paint the bread and hen.
- Glue the feathers to the hen.
- Use twisted pipe cleaners for the legs

animals

- Cut out the pig and paint with a mixture of pink paint and sand.
- Cut out the dog and cat and cover with fur.
- Use buttons for eyes.
- Decorate with ribbons.
- Windmill: cut out a windmill shape and use lolly sticks to give a wood effect.
- Glue art straws to the sails.
- Use a wooden wheel for turning the sails
- Border: children's cut out handprints.

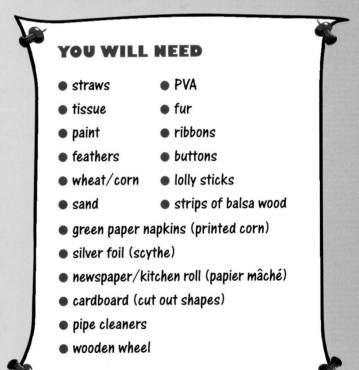

YOU WILL NEED

- straws
- tissue
- paint
- feathers
- wheat/corn
- sand
- PVA
- fur
- ribbons
- buttons
- lolly sticks
- strips of balsa wood
- green paper napkins (printed corn)
- silver foil (scythe)
- newspaper/kitchen roll (papier mâché)
- cardboard (cut out shapes)
- pipe cleaners
- wooden wheel

YOU WILL NEED

- paper – backing, sugar and shiny
- paint
- fabric
- black tissue paper
- tin foil or foil cake cases
- egg boxes
- salt dough
- pva
- apple box tray
- string
- glitter and sand
- kitchen rolls
- pipe cleaners
- branches
- corrugated cardboard
- cotton wool
- net
- pompoms
- cellophane

approach

Use green and blue backing paper for sky and grass

Mary is made from fabric.

Handprints form flowers. Cut and stick yellow centres.

Silver bells are made from egg box sections covered in silver foil.

Flowers along the fence are made from salt dough painted and varnished.

Pond – cut and stick bits of shiny paper.

Butterflies – blobs of paint and fold to create symmetrical pattern.

Watering can painted silver.

Clouds and water are made from cellophane.

Cockle shells – foil cut to a shell shape, glue on glitter and sand.

Fence – painted corrugated card.

Bees

Paint kitchen roll tube yellow.

Add smiley face.

Pipe cleaner legs.

Add black stripes.

Pleat netting for wings.

Pompom head.

Wrap cotton wool with black tissue to make a sting.

Salt Dough Recipe

1. 1 cup salt

2. 1 cup flour

3. 1/2 cup water

4. mix together

Poetry in Windows

windows

The idea of using windows to stimulate children's curiosity can be used in subjects other than poetry. Children have to open the window to discover what lies beneath!

ocean poems

In this instance the theme was 'The Ocean' and therefore the character 'embracing' the children's work is an octopus.

The idea of a character from the topic studied being enlarged to be the backdrop of the display could be used in any subject.

good/bad poems

The idea for this theme came from *'A Poetry Teacher's Toolkit Book 3: Style, Shape and Structure'* by Collette Drifle and Mike Jubb (Fulton 2002)

Children are encouraged to think of a subject then write some 'good things' and some 'not so good things.'

Children have great fun creating these poems.

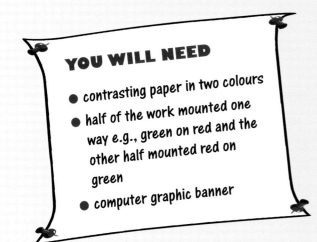

YOU WILL NEED

- contrasting paper in two colours
- half of the work mounted one way e.g., green on red and the other half mounted red on green
- computer graphic banner

DREAMER

POEMS

The stimulus was a poem by Brian Moses 'The Dreamer'

> *I dreamt I was a chair*
> *but no one sat on me.*
> *I dreamt I was a cup*
> *but no one drank from me.*

approach

- Children look up 'dream' in a thesaurus and type labels, which are synonyms.

- The display of the children's work attempts to reflect the theme of 'dreams'. The back of a girl's head is the central feature and from it circles are used to create 'thoughts'. Each piece of work is mounted in a 'thought bubble'.

Creating cloud effects

This idea is very simple but effective. The 'ANGELS' display was produced as a result of the children (aged 10-11) studying a class novel, *'Slellig' by David Almond.* The children were asked to write a description or a poem of their own 'angel' found in an unusual place.

approach

- On purple backing paper create a cloud effect by spraying around a stencil shape of a cloud.

- Add silver border.

- Mount poems on silver and black paper cut to create a cloud shape.

- Title: stencils and letters cut out in silver.

- Arrange work and title.

YOU WILL NEED

- purple backing paper
- silver border roll
- silver spray paint
- silver and black mounting paper

Warning

- Use a mask when using spray paint.
- Do not use if asthmatic.

21

word banks

High frequency words/key words children should know are often displayed on classroom walls or chalkboards. As these are changed throughout the year it is a good idea to have a display that can remain, so that you change only the words.

YOU WILL NEED

- black, red and cream backing paper
- gold paper for title and bookmark
- card for words
- laminate for word cards
- Velcro

approach

- The key words to be used are written on card and laminated.

- They are attached to the display with Velcro.

- Children are encouraged to use the key words on their writing. They remove a word from the display to copy and then replace it on the display.

- Examples of children's work that include the key words are displayed opposite the words.

- Individual or pairs of children are encouraged to read the piece of writing and identify the key words.

The Word Eating Dragon is used as a cumulative word bank. It can be used for high frequency words or high interest words from the big book being used. Each week, words are fed into the dragon. A different colour can be used for each week's words, so you can monitor carefully the children's use of the words in their writing.

The display can be used to remind children of the words they have learned during whole class sessions. It also acts as a reference tool for the children when they are writing.

approach

- Cut out a cardboard template of a dragon.

- Cut and stick textured paper onto the body.

- Cut and stick wings and spikes to the body.

- Make the eyes and mouth from egg boxes and ping pong balls.

- Sponge paint bricks.

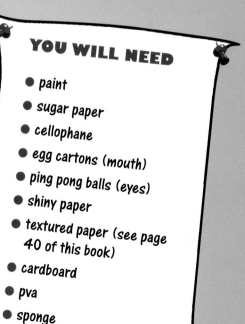

YOU WILL NEED

- paint
- sugar paper
- cellophane
- egg cartons (mouth)
- ping pong balls (eyes)
- shiny paper
- textured paper (see page 40 of this book)
- cardboard
- pva
- sponge

f.f.fish

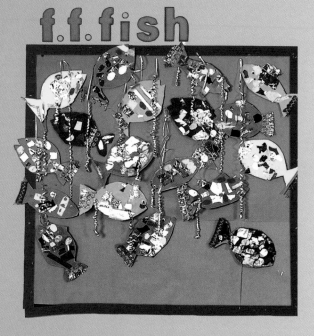

words beginning with...

You may decide to concentrate on one letter a week with very young children.

approach

- Start with one word e.g. fish and ask children to make their own fish for the display.

- Talk about other words beginning with 'f'.

- Make up silly sentences with as many 'f' words as they can think of e.g. *Five foolish fishermen went fishing for frogs (feet, feathers.....)*

other ideas

Letter displays can also be used to teach colours and numbers

- **Counting** - consecutive numbers

- **Questioning** - how many teddies have red waistcoats?

- **Matching** - How many pairs have matching waistcoats and bow ties?

t.t.teddy

s.s.snake

YOU WILL NEED

- templates of fish, teddies and snakes
- paper for children to cut up could be sweet wrappings, foil, sticky paper
- glue

weather words

What is the weather today?
What is the weather today?

It's cold and wet,
It's cold and wet,
That is the weather today.

What is the weather today?
What is the weather today?

It's warm and dry,
It's warm and dry,
That is the weather today.

Today it is Thursday

Today it is **cloudy**

months of the year

Months of the year		
January	1	
February	2	
March	3	
April	4	
May	5	
June	6	
July	7	
August	8	
September	9	
October	10	
November	11	
December	12	

days of the week

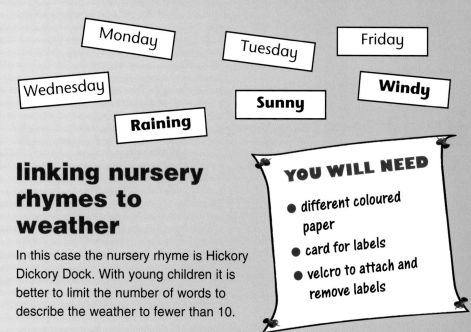

Monday

Tuesday

Friday

Wednesday

Windy

Sunny

Raining

linking nursery rhymes to weather

In this case the nursery rhyme is Hickory Dickory Dock. With young children it is better to limit the number of words to describe the weather to fewer than 10.

YOU WILL NEED

● different coloured paper
● card for labels
● velcro to attach and remove labels

25

Rama and the Demon King

The Story of Rama and Sita

The stimulus for the display and work with puppets was the book 'Rama and the Demon King' by Jessica Sonhami. The story of Rama and Sita and their battle with the many headed demon king, Ravana, is a popular story with children. It is usually studied when investigating myths and legends. Rama and Sita is an ancient Indian myth. The characters surrounding the demon king are animals who helped Rama.

The children have written a summary of the story around the sleeves and edge of Ravana's outfit.

YOU WILL NEED

- bright poster paper
- black sugar paper
- sequins
- odd bits of material, feather etc. for decoration.

approach

- Add the body to the display first.
- Children draw around their hands and cut them out. Add to the display
- Ten children make the ten heads.
- Other children make the animals.
- Make the labels for main characters using a large font on a computer

Shadow puppets

You might use commercially produced shadow puppets to reenact the story.

Rama and Ravana shadow puppets.

The shadow puppets behind the screen are very effective.

Children made Ravana's army as puppets.

YOU WILL NEED

- black sugar paper
- wood dowelling
- white strips of paper
- staples

approach

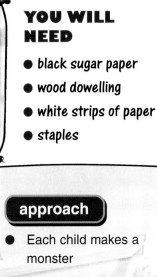

- Each child makes a monster

- Mount these on a mobile. This acts as a backdrop to the battle between Ravana and Rama

FINGER PUPPETS

First of all we had to look at puppets that we brought in from home. Then we had to find out what they were made of and how they were fixed together.

Next we had to complete a practical task where we practised how to join fabrics together.
We used glue, staples, sellotape, paper clips and elastic bands.

After that we had to design our finger puppet thinking about which tools and materials we were going to use.

YOU WILL NEED
- made puppets
- felt
- buttons/sequins
- cotton
- needles

Do you think that you can design your own puppet?

My design

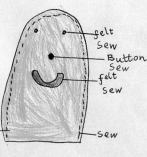

- felt — Sew
- Button — Sew
- felt — Sew
- felt
- Sew

Finally we made our puppets thinking about the final product and how it was going to look.

Displaying finger puppets with the designs

Designing A Puppet...

In Design and Technology we have been making puppets.

YOU WILL NEED

- backed board
- curtain fabric
- bought puppets
- computer graphics
- children's puppets.

approach

- In design and technology the children designed and made their own puppets.

- Each puppet is displayed next to its design

- The displays on this page are examples of two ways to display pupils' work

Our Puppets

We looked at puppets to see how the parts were fixed together

We tried out different ways of fixing materials

We designed our puppets and decided which materials and tools to use. We practised some skills-drawing around a template, cutting and sewing

We made some wonderful finger puppets. We evaluated our work to see how we could improve our designing and making skills

puppet theatres

Commercially produced puppet theatres can be purchased quite cheaply. The range of puppets available is vast.

three-way puppets

Particularly wonderful for story telling are puppets that consist of three characters in one.

make your own puppet theatre

This is a simple idea that a pair or a small group of children can readily design and make.

approach

- Cover a whole cardboard box with coloured paper and paint on a design. This forms the base.

- Cut out the front of a second box to create a stage.

- Cut away the top of the box so that puppets can be lowered onto the stage.

- Paint different backdrops to create different scenes form the story.

- Design a curtain that drops or one that slides to each side.

- Make the characters and attach a piece of dowel vertically to the back of each character. The dowel should extend at least 20cm above the head for the child to hold.

YOU WILL NEED

- 2 similar-sized cardboard boxes
- dowel
- paint
- coloured paper
- curtain material
- string of elastic to hang the curtain

BURSTING OUT OF BORDERS

Displays can look really exciting and different if you consider overlapping the border with the children's work or taking the theme as a background shape, as in the sunflowers display.

Sunflowers

Van Gogh's 'Sunflowers' was used as a stimulus. The children were asked to create sunflowers with texture using pastels.

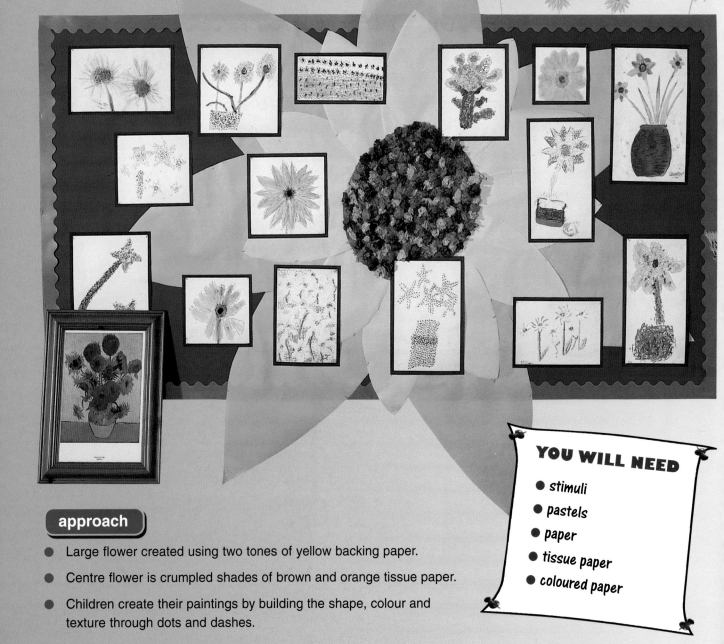

approach

- Large flower created using two tones of yellow backing paper.
- Centre flower is crumpled shades of brown and orange tissue paper.
- Children create their paintings by building the shape, colour and texture through dots and dashes.

YOU WILL NEED

- stimuli
- pastels
- paper
- tissue paper
- coloured paper

communication board

*I just wanted to say…….*can be displayed throughout the year. It gives the children the opportunity to write their comments. These may be for other children, the whole class, adults or general comments about what they have been doing. Some weeks the children or the teacher might decide on the theme, for example three themes used in this class have been *'September 11th'*, *'Moving class'* and *'Welcoming a new child'*.

I just wanted to say…… Thanks for a great day you are a terrific class. Mr. Brown

I just wanted to say…… To Yurik Welcome to our class. James

I just wanted to say…… Have a happy birthday Mike. Jo

YOU WILL NEED

- backing paper
- photocopies of speech bubbles
- pins
- drawn characters

approach

- Provide speech bubbles for the children to write comments on.
- Cartoon characters make the display more exciting.
- Read through as a class at the end of Friday.
- Start with a clean board on Monday.

I just wanted to say …

ALL ABOUT ME

approach

As part of the Personal, Social and Health Education topic children were asked to consider 'who we are' and 'where we belong'. In designing a poster they identified different categories such as places, events, things they are proud of, etc. Under each category they then had to list 5 words or statements. Sarah's is a good example of creativity. The border is made of hand and footprints.

YOU WILL NEED

- card
- photographs
- string
- paper
- paint
- felt tips
- scissors

Networks

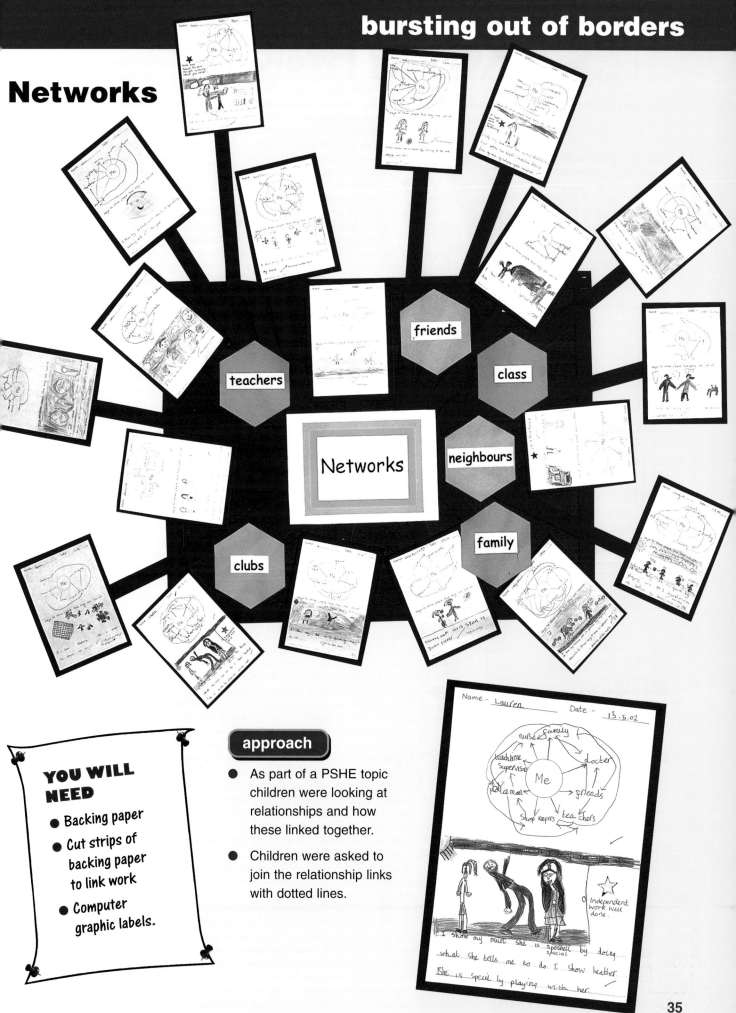

approach

- As part of a PSHE topic children were looking at relationships and how these linked together.

- Children were asked to join the relationship links with dotted lines.

YOU WILL NEED

- Backing paper
- Cut strips of backing paper to link work
- Computer graphic labels.

friends

class

teachers

Networks

neighbours

clubs

family

Name:- Lauren   Date:- 15.5.02

35

Keeping Healthy

Carbohydrates
Carbohydrates: energy giving foods, such as potatoes, pasta, bread

Vitamins
Vitamins: an organic compound which is essential for good health, found in foods such as fruit and vegetables.

Protein
Protein: a substance which is essential for growth and repair, found in foods such as meat, fish and cheese.

Sugars
Sugars: a group of sweet-tasting carbohydrates

Fats
Fats: made of glycerol and fatty acids, needed for energy

DESIGNING A SANDWICH

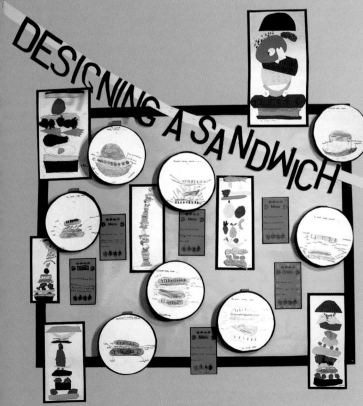

A balanced diet

Children designed healthy eating menus and healthy sandwiches using the main food groups.

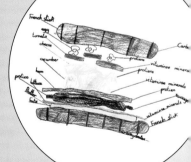

approach

- The sandwich designs are mounted on circular black paper.

- A strip of card is stapled to the back of the circle at the top.

- Bend back the strip of paper and staple to the wall.

Smile please

approach

- The display was produced as part of a science topic 'Looking after our teeth'. Children were asked to design posters. The 3 dimensional mouth at the centre was created:

- Draw teeth on to white card.

- Staple each section of the mouth to the display board whilst filling it with newspaper to make it 3D.

- Finish the display by adding the children's posters

YOU WILL NEED

- red material
- newspaper
- white card
- photocopied teeth border
- black marker pen

Creative Backgrounds

Interesting backgrounds can be made at very low cost and yet be very effective.

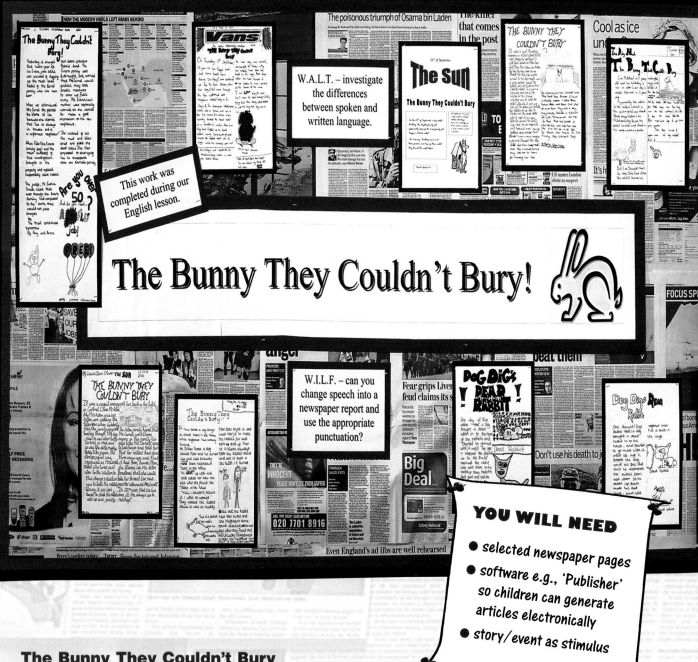

The Bunny They Couldn't Bury

The focus of the topic was looking at writing for different purposes, specifically at changing an oral account into a newspaper report.

The outcome is children writing an article for a newspaper.

The background for the display is, appropriately, pages from a newspaper.

Other Ideas

Use popular magazines as stimulus for children writing an article about a celebrity.

Comics could be used as stimulus to writing creative reports 'My Interview with Denis the Menace!'

Who was John Lennon ?

The children (aged 10-11) were studying popular culture in the 1960s as part of their history topic. They looked at the life of John Lennon. The background is repeated pictures of John Lennon.

approach

- Cover the board with pictures of John Lennon.
- Children make small discs from silver and gold paper for the border.
- Children paint the large colourful John Lennon as a centre piece.
- They paint large guitars.
- The children's written work is placed around John Lennon.

YOU WILL NEED

- photocopies of John Lennon or your chosen celebrity
- large card
- black card
- gold and silver stars
- paint
- silver and gold paper

Backing with a difference

Commercially produced backing paper has gone a long way since plain coloured sugar paper.
You can now obtain backing paper with a textured design.

The mountain lion

Mountain lions glinting
eyes are visible through a bril-
liant green bush,
The sound of a bee is drawing closer though I'm not defi-
nite .Might it be a humming
bird of a cerise pink?
Eerie splashes are coming
from the watering hole,
Shadows are scurrying
around silently, as galloping
hooves of Zebra can be heard.
The mountain peak is
glowing as the golden sun
rises.

By Kimberley Aston

These are four examples of interesting backgrounds. They are obtainable from School Suppliers.

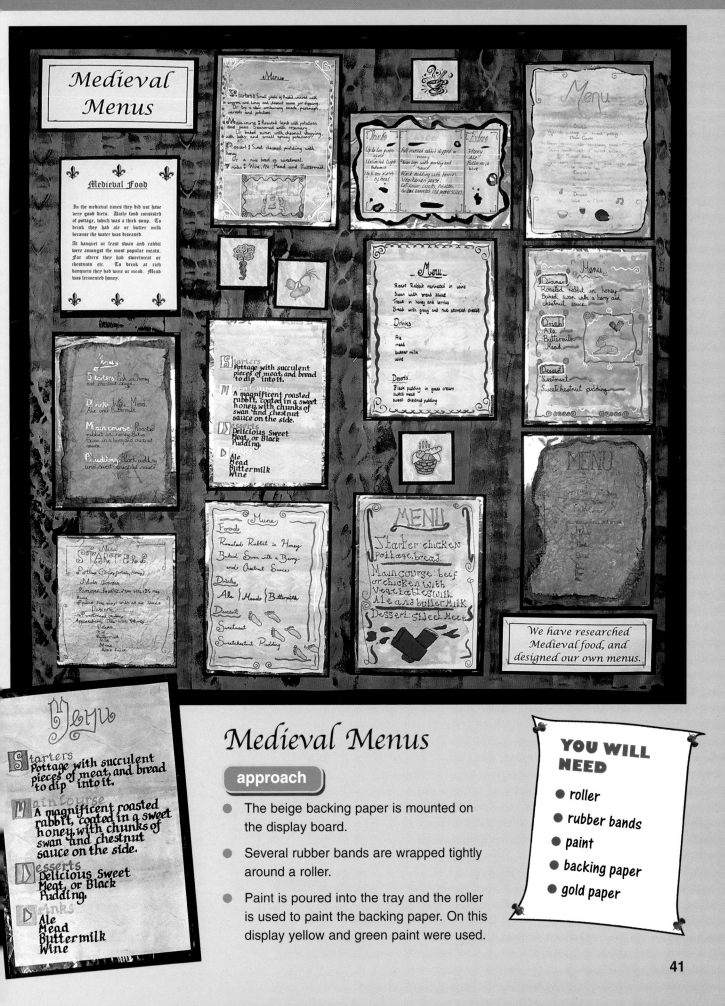

Medieval Menus

approach

- The beige backing paper is mounted on the display board.

- Several rubber bands are wrapped tightly around a roller.

- Paint is poured into the tray and the roller is used to paint the backing paper. On this display yellow and green paint were used.

YOU WILL NEED

- roller
- rubber bands
- paint
- backing paper
- gold paper

41

painted backgrounds

Children can be creative and have fun designing backgrounds for the displays that match the topic.

landscapes

This was an art topic with 10-11 year olds.

stimulus

The work of different artists: Oskar Kokoschka - Polperro II,
Pieter Bruegel - Haymaking, Rubens - The Rainbow Landscape,
Travel brochures and postcards

approach

- Cover the board with black sugar paper.

- Use small squares of corrugated card dipped in thick green
  paint to create background.

- Make window mounts from black card.

- Arrange children's work with two central lines
  going out from the middle of the board. Illustrate

YOU WILL NEED

- black sugar paper
- small squares of corrugated card
- coloured pencils
- watercolour paints
- black card
- green border roll
- paint tray

Dreamtime stories

As part of their literacy topic the children (aged 10-11) were studying Australian dreamtime stories.

Children created their own Aboriginal paintings for the background to display their own dreamtime stories.

approach

- The children used wax crayons and pastels to create Aboriginal paintings on beige cartridge paper.

- They illustrated dreamtime stories they found on the web. These were read aloud to the class.

- The lettering is drawn and cut out and attached to the display.

YOU WILL NEED

- beige cartridge paper
- wax crayons
- oil pastels
- corrugated card
- orange shades of mounting paper
- A4 coloured paper
- curly border roll.

The Great Fire

In Literacy we have been learning about different styles of writing. We now understand that we write for different audiences and purposes.

When we wrote our pieces of writing we had to try and imagine what Samuel Pepys might have seen, heard and smelt.

We have been learning about The Great Fire of London that happened in 1666.

Samuel Pepys wrote a diary and in it he wrote all about this tragic event.

In this piece of work we had to write as if we were Samuel Pepys. We had to write in the first person which can be quite difficult to remember.

Tuesday 4th September 1666.

The fire was raging the pigeons fell from the sky with burnt feathers. Cats and dogs are running. King Charles said pull down the house. People buried things like gold and silver in their garden. Some people went in wooden boats to try to escape the fire. But the river got on fire and the boat got hotter and hotter. Back in London the children and the mummies and daddies are shouting screaming and the fire spread. I could smell the fire and I could smell the flames. I was a bit terrified and the people were very scared.

Children looked at extracts from Samuel Pepys' Diary when studying the 'Fire of London'. His eye-witness account of the fire was the stimulus for a shared reading activity.

YOU WILL NEED

- black and white picture of the fire of london
- red backing paper
- red, yellow and orange paper
- A3 white paper
- coffee and water to stain the paper
- orange, yellow, red and black paint
- silver paper

# of London

The display shows words mounted on silver paper arranged around a painted silhouette of the London skyline on fire:

What did the people...

Panic, Chaos, See, Flames, Mess, Death, Burning, Food, Smell, Wood, Gun Powder, Screaming, Crackling, Hear, Shouting, Splashing, Exploding

approach

Samuel Pepys' diary

- Make multiple photocopies of the picture to use as backing paper.

- The children cut out different size flames from the orange, red and yellow paper.

- The children's diary extracts, written from the point of view of Samuel Pepys, are enlarged to A3 and stained with coffee and water mix.

- Put the writing in an oven to dry and change colour.

- Rip around the edge.

- Mount the writing on backing paper and rip around the edge again.

What did the people...

- The children considered what the people who saw the Fire of London would have seen, heard and smelled.

- After brainstorming the words that best describe the events, the children produced the words on computer for the display. These are mounted on silver paper.

- Colour paint wash is used for the sky and left to dry.

- A silhouette of the skyline is painted on the red sky.

Think **Big**

The Divided Lovers
A Tale from Japan

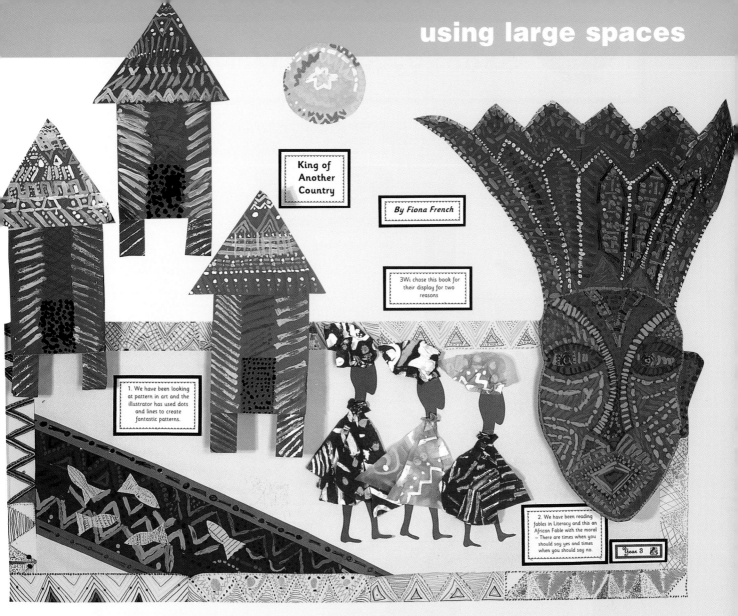

King of Another Country

By Fiona French

3Wi chose this book for their display for two reasons

1. We have been looking at pattern in art and the illustrator has used dots and lines to create fantastic patterns.

2. We have been reading fables in Literacy and this an African Fable with the moral – There are times when you should say yes and times when you should say no.

Year 3

Displays on large areas are best kept simple.

The Divided Lovers

The story can be found in "Sun, Moon and Stars" by Mary Hoffman and Jane Ray published by Orion.

YOU WILL NEED

- backing paper
- tissues
- cartridge paper
- objects to print with e.g., strips of card, cotton reels
- paint
- border strips
- feathers
- gold felt tip
- silver and gold paper

King of Another Country

The class art topic was 'Pattern'. The children (aged 7-8) looked at a whole range of patterns in the environment and on animals. The book chosen to study during book week was 'King of Another Country' by Fiona French.

approach

- Group the children to work on different sections of the display.

- Large head: print on pencil drawing of god. Children decide on patterns.

- River: individual children printed patterns on strips of cards in shades of blue.

- Huts: method same as the river in natural shades

- People: cut out head, legs and arms. Bright coloured twine used for clothes.

- Border: yellow border strip with thick felt tip patterns.

Spooky, Scary Writing

Descriptive Writing

Poems and extracts from fiction books were shared with the class as examples of descriptive writing. The display has been created to reflect the theme.

approach

- Back the display with black sugar paper

- Wrap rubber bands around the roller

- Roll roller in tray of white paint and move across the black sugar paper keeping the direction the same. This creates the background.

- The banner was produced in 'Publisher'

- Mount finished work on black sugar paper.

YOU WILL NEED

- Black sugar paper
- Small roller
- Rubber bands
- Paint tray
- Thick white paint

Instructional text

The children (aged 7-8) read instructional texts, identified common features and discussed different layouts. Before looking at some text they considered what the reader would need and then assessed whether the text did this. They then followed instructions to make a Roman scroll.

YOU WILL NEED

- A4 paper
- Ribbon
- Wooden sticks
- Brown powder paint
- Set of instructions
- PVA

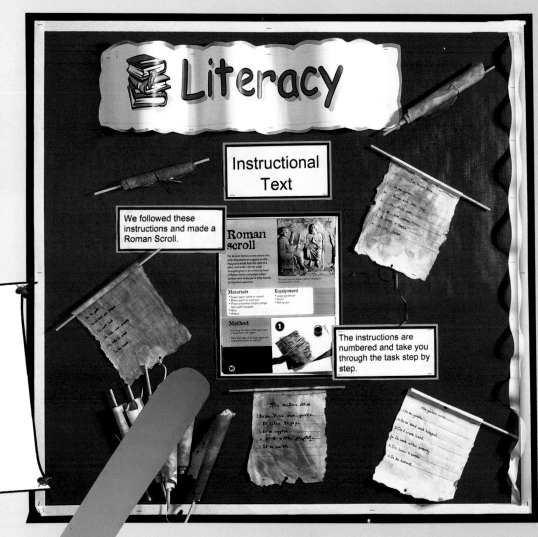

approach

- children follow the instructions
- a stick is glued to the top of the finished work
- a length of ribbon is attached to the bottom
- a mixture of powder paint and water is used as a colour wash on the white paper
- display at different angles, some rolled up.

Letter writing

This is a very simple idea that can be used with any age group.

The title has been produced on the computer. A large envelope and pencil have been cut out of green sugar paper to form part of the frame.

the writers' timeline

Timelines are usually associated with history topics but they have a wider potential.
This is also a project that the whole school can contribute to.

approach

- At the beginning of the school term start the display by putting up the timeline to cover the period of the subject you are using.

- Decide how you will divide the time. In this example two thirds of the timeline is devoted to the 20th Century.

- As each class or pupil reads a book, that title is placed on the timeline along with associated pupil work. Books, book covers and dust jackets can be displayed.

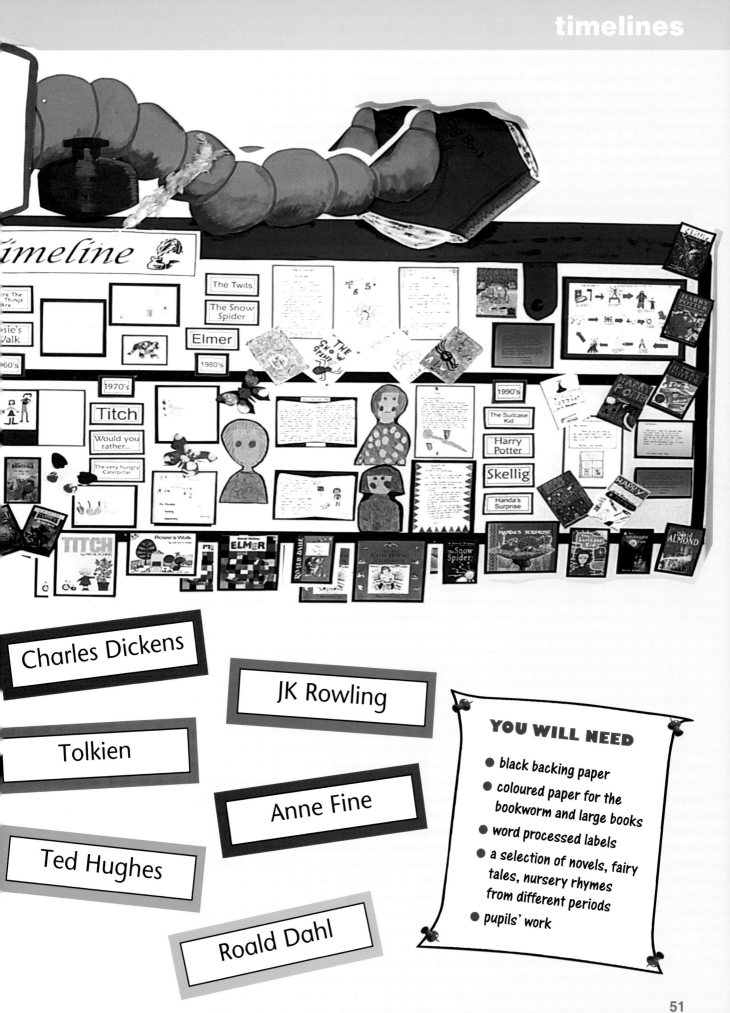

Charles Dickens

JK Rowling

Tolkien

Anne Fine

Ted Hughes

Roald Dahl

YOU WILL NEED

- black backing paper
- coloured paper for the bookworm and large books
- word processed labels
- a selection of novels, fairy tales, nursery rhymes from different periods
- pupils' work

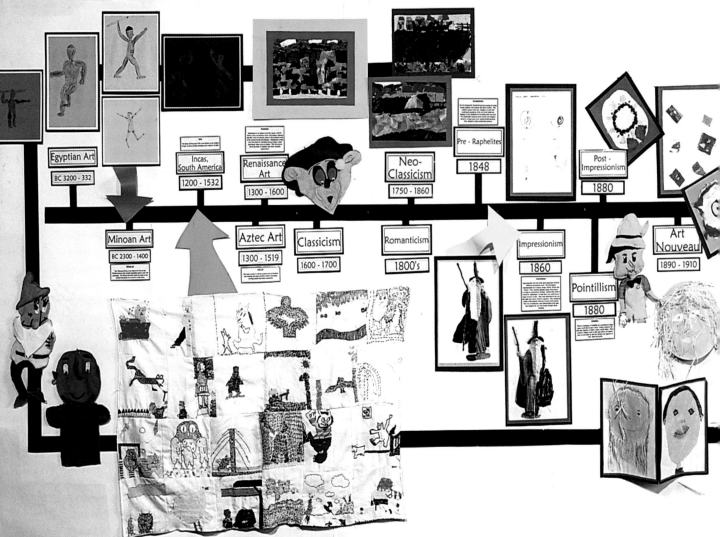

the artists' timeline

This is a similar idea to the Writers' Timeline on pages 50/51. It too can be a whole school display that can be added to throughout the term or year.

This timeline begins with Egyptian art and runs through different periods up to the present day. In each case the children's' work is in the style of a particular period or of an individual artist that they have studied. The labels and written work were produced using a word processor.

YOU WILL NEED

- a large communal area that will be available all year. A corridor is ideally suited.
- stimuli such as photographs, books and art reproductions from the period or artist studied.
- a wide range of media including paint, pastels, charcoal, crayon, inks etc.
- backing paper
- labels

Cubism
1907

Abstract
Expressionism
1940 - 1960

Conceptual
Art
1970

Expressionism
1906

Surrealism
1920 - 1930

Pop Art
1960

Contemporary
Art

Present Day

Push the
boat out

YOU WILL NEED

- felt
- needles
- cotton

Consider using the school entrance as the 'Art Gallery'. The work of individual children can be taken from classrooms and displayed here for a whole variety of reasons. Glass cabinets display smaller three-dimensional pieces to excellent effect. Glass clip frames are used to display artwork indicating the high value the school places on presentation.

Gemma Jones A GREEK URN

George Cornwell A GRECIAN URN

Children design their own labels on the computer.

display competition

Let the children decide what should go in the Art Gallery or which class display is to be the chosen winner each term.

approach

- When a class has completed a display the members of the class decide if it is worthy to be entered for the 'Class Display Competition'.

- All entries have to be in by a specified closing date.

- Every class in the school completes a 'Display Judging Sheet' . In this example there are six criteria (statements) and the class can award a score of 1, 2 or 3.

- The criteria and the scores should be decided by the children.

DISPLAY JUDGING SHEET

Please return to Mr. McHugh by Thursday 22nd

DISPLAY COMPETITION: SUMMER

FROM CLASS:

STATEMENTS:
1. The display is interactive.
2. The quality of writing is good for the year group.
3. The artwork for the year group.
4. The display is easy to understand.
5. The display is eye-catching.
6. I like the display.

SCORING
Nearly all the class agree 3
Approximately half the class agrees 2
Fewer than half agree 1

Display Name	Statements 1	Statements 2	Statements 3	Statements 4	Statements 5	Statements 6	Total
Pilgrim CLASS 6							
Lord of the Rings CLASS 5							
Shadows CLASS 4							
Our Bodies CLASS 7							
The Egyptians CLASS 3							
Where we Live CLASS 2							

THE WINNER IS:

Best Display

The overall winning display , decided by the whole school, is identified and given a gold star award.

moving toys

The background for this display represents a moving toy and shows a linear cam. Each piece of work is mounted on a frame that reflects the design.

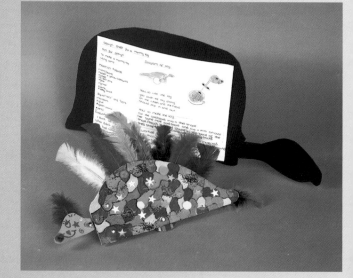

approach

- Draw the background by freehand or using an OHP.

- Children design their own toy and complete their design sheet. The headings are:

  - Design sheet for moving toy
  - Aim of design
  - Materials required
  - Equipment and tools
  - Evaluation
  - Diagram of the toy
  - How to use the toy
  - How to make the toy

- The made toy is displayed on the surface and its design sheet is displayed on a black, silhouette frame that reflects the toy design.

- The materials you will need will depend on the children's designs.

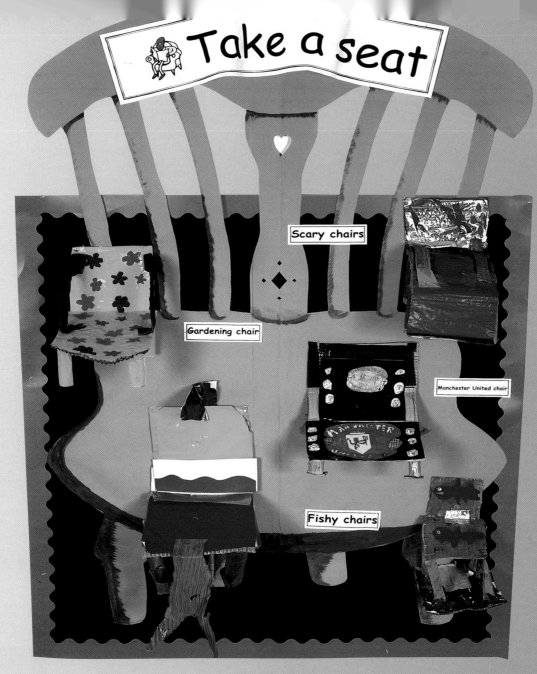

Take a seat

Scary chairs

Gardening chair

Manchester United chair

Fishy chairs

take a seat

The background for the display reflects the theme.

YOU WILL NEED

- Backing paper
- Drawing materials e.g. medium grade graphite pencils, coloured pencils
- Materials for construction e.g. card, glue, double-sided tape, stapler
- Paint
- Sketch books
- Coloured paper

approach

- Draw the background by freehand or using an OHP.
- The children look at seats used in different places, times, by different cultures and for different purposes:

  - **Mass use** e.g. schools, offices, theatres.
  - **In the home** e.g. kitchen chair, sofa, armchair
  - **Outside** e.g. garden furniture, park bench
  - **Transport** e.g. buses, planes, ship

Children design a seat for their chosen purpose and label it.

MOVING STORYBOOK PAGES

Children make up their own stories that involve the movement of characters or objects. They then design and make these moving structures. In addition to being a design opportunity children are writing with purpose and for an audience.

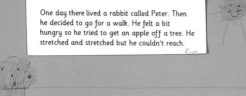

One day there lived a rabbit called Peter. Then he decided to go for a walk. He felt a bit hungry so he tried to get an apple off a tree. He stretched and stretched but he couldn't reach.

One day there lived a rabbit called Peter. Then he decided to go for a walk. He felt a bit hungry so he tried to get an apple off a tree. He stretched and stretched but he couldn't reach.

↓ ↓ PULL ↓

approach

- The children investigate linkage-type mechanism using levers and pivots.

- They use a step by step design sheet similar to the one on page 56.

- The final product is evaluated and modifications suggested.

YOU WILL NEED

- Card
- Paper
- Glue
- Scissors
- Paper fasteners
- Crayons
- Word processor for the stories.

One starry night an astronaut came to the moon. He knew everything about the moon but the only thing he did not know about the moon was that there was an alien living on it. Well when the astronaut got there an alien came up to him and said come with me so the astronaut did. But what the astronaut did not know was that the alien had a special drink that would turn the astronaut into an alien. So when he drank it he turned into an alien.

One starry night an astronaut came to the moon. He knew everything about the moon but the only thing he did not know about the moon was that there was an alien living on it. Well when the astronaut got there an alien came up to him and said come with me so the astronaut did. But what the astronaut did not know was that the alien had a special drink that would turn the astronaut into an alien. So when he drank it he turned into an alien.

↓ PULL ↓

MAKING MUSIC

making music

The children design a musical instrument and then make it. The design sheet categories are similar to those given on page 56. The display illustrates both the designs and the finished pieces. In this case the background of the musical note reflects the theme. It breaks up the border and provides an eye-catching display.

approach

- Draw the background by freehand or using an OHP.

- Tie string across the front of the display to hold some of the musical instruments.

- Place boxes under the throw to display finished designs at different heights.

- The children's musical instruments are displayed on the surfaces and their designs are pinned to the board.

YOU WILL NEED

- Backing paper
- Black paper for musical notes and borders
- String
- A plain throw
- Small boxes
- A range of drawing and construction materials as on page 57
- A range of containers, plastic bottles, tins , boxes.

Local Traffic Study
Our School Car Park

private transport

public transport

No spaces!

pollution

congestion

Danger!

walk

too many cars!

ride

Parking

Identifying issues for study that are within the children's personal experiences is widely recognised as good practice. Parking is an issue for many schools especially at the beginning and end of the school day.

approach

- Display board is backed.

- Strips of white and yellow paper are used for parking bays and/or parking restrictions.

- The children draw and paint large cars for the parking bays.

- The children's work (opposite) can be placed around the display.

YOU WILL NEED

- Backing paper
- Silver or grey paper
- Paint
- Large card
- Word processor for letter writing and labels

60

approach

- Children start by looking at the problems associated with school parking.

- They survey the views of different users.

- They identify possible solutions.

- They make signs for the car park.

- In pairs or groups the children redesign the car park using the information gathered.

- Letters are written to the town council to raise awareness of the problem. These letters can be word processed or hand written.

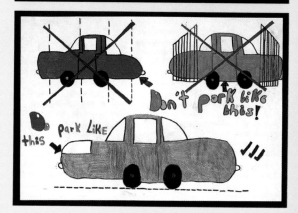

How to play-
Can you say what
you would do in
these situations?

Look under the
picture and see
the correct
answer.

What would you do?

drowning

Car crash

burglary

Building site

fire

Hazard Alley

The display is a result of children's work on safety.
They visited the imaginary 'Hazard Alley' where they
were faced with emergency situations. They discussed
with adults what dangers they faced and what
appropriate actions they should take such as ringing
the emergency services and giving a name and
location.

STOP

YOU WILL NEED

- Large sheets of paper
- Pastels
- Paint
- Backing paper
- Red paper for signs
- Word processor for labels
  and situation reports.

Lift picture

"If you come across someone in the water you go straight to a phone box and call 999 for the emergency services. Don't forget to give your name and details of were you are."
by Amarda Clarke

How to play-
Can you say what you would do in these situations?

Look under the picture and see the correct answer.

approach

- Children work in pairs.

- One draws a picture of a hazardous situation (e.g. a child in water) and the picture is laminated.

- The second child uses the word processor to write what to do in such a situation.

- Appropriate responses are displayed on the board.

- The laminated picture is placed in front of the writing.

- Two pieces of card are used as hinges so the picture can be lifted to reveal the writing.

- Individual children make safety signs for the border

- In pairs, children look at a picture, discuss or write what they would do in that situation and then lift the picture to compare their response to the one on the display.

- An extension activity is to ask children to draw or paint safe places in the local area.

Sculpture

We have looked at sculpture around Milton Keynes and the works by Claes Oldenberg on the Internet.

What do you think of these ideas for a huge sculpture outside the library?

Sculpture

The stimulus for the children's work was sculpture in the local area and the work of famous sculptors.

approach

- Children collect postcards or take photographs of local sculptures.

- Children look at the work of famous sculptors using books and the Internet.

- Sculptors who inspired this work:

  - Claes Oldenburg inspired the paper sculpture.

  - Wassily Kandinsky inspired the work on tiles.

- The work of local artists inspired the clay sculptures of people and animals.

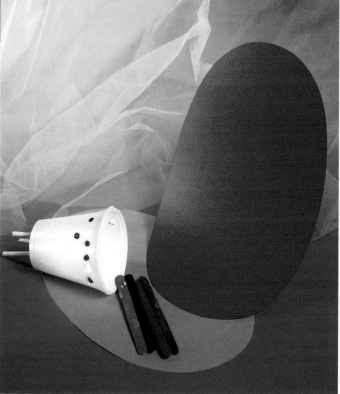

CLAY MODELS
- Newclay
- Rolling pin
- Wooden boards
- Modelling tools
- Paint

SCULPTURES
- Tissue
- Straws
- Sticks
- Coloured paper
- Polystyrene cups
- Glue
- Small boxes

approach

- Children make sculptures from a range of materials available. The list provided here is not exhaustive.

- The 'Newclay' used for the tiles and models does not need firing and therefore can be used without a kiln.

- The display shows models that have yet to be painted and others that have been finished.

PAPER SCULPTURE

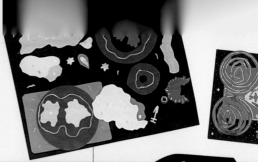

The stimulus for these two displays was wooden sculptures around the school that children had designed and that had subsequently been created by a local sculptor.

approach

- Children look at the sculptures around the school, focusing specifically on the use of line.

- They design their own sculptures.

- Using paper they make their sculptures

labelling the display

- Cut the corrugated paper to size.

- Spray with silver paint.

- Spray straws with gold paint.

- Stick the straws onto the corrugated paper to make the letters.

YOU WILL NEED

- A wide range of coloured paper
- Corrugated card
- Silver and gold spray paint
- Straws   ● Paint
- Small stars ● Glue

warning

- Eye protection should be worn when using spray paint

- Children should be supervised by an adult when spraying

- Anyone with asthma or other respiratory problems should not be involved.

YOU WILL NEED

- Paper
- Tissue
- Glue
- Egg cartons
- Ribbon

Easter Bonnets

Every child in the school was given the opportunity to design and make a hat for an 'Easter Parade'.

approach

- Children need help in making the hat to appropriate size.

67

Airmiles

The 'Airmiles' idea is based on a whole school approach to 'Golden Time' . It is an approach based on incentives linked to the school's 'Golden Rules'. To participate in special activities offered during Golden Time children need to abide by the Golden Rules.

GOLDEN RULES

Do be gentle

Do be kind and helpful

Do work hard

Do look after property

Do listen to people

Do be honest

Do not hurt anybody

Do not hurt anyone's feelings

Do not waste your or other people's time

Do not waste or damage things

Do not cover up the truth

approach

- Children are divided into groups known as the 'Airline Crew'.

- The pilot and co-pilot are chosen.

- They act as managers of the 'Cabin Crew' and ensure all the crew are ready at all times.

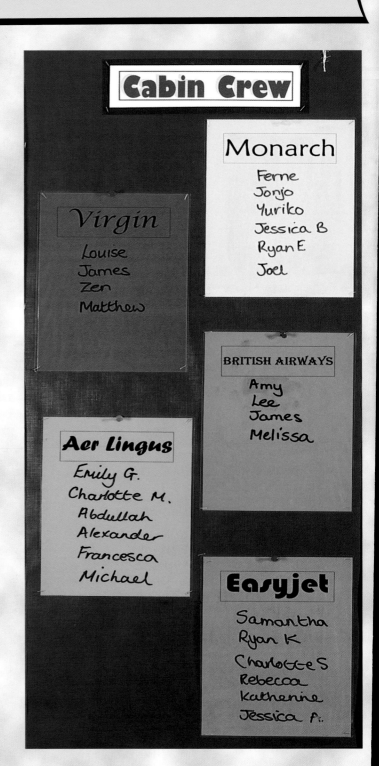

Step 1

Choose a destination using an atlas. Work out the distance in miles using the intranet. Record this information on your airline report card

Step 2

Follow the golden rules by working hard and behaving well. Keep your tables tidy and flight packs clean. You will be rewarded with airmiles

Step 3

Every two weeks add up your airmiles. If you have reached your destination you may go to passport control. Have your passport stamped and choose your next destination

Step 4

Your aim is to travel the world and get the highest travel score

Flight packs

Each group (airline) has a flight pack on their table. This contains everyday items such as pencils, rulers, crayons, felt tips, glue. It is the pilot and co-pilot's responsibility to make sure their 'Cabin Crew' keep their 'Flight Deck' tidy and ready for action.

destination day

● Every two weeks crews have a 'Destination Day'. They use atlases to choose a destination and the Internet to calculate the distance. This becomes the crew's target for the next two weeks.

● They can gain air miles for: getting ready, finishing work, good behaviour etc.

● They record the air miles they are awarded and at the end of two weeks count up the total and check if they can reach their destination.

Air Miles Record and Travel Score

up to 500miles = 5points

500 - 1000miles = 10points

1000 - 2000miles =20 points

2000 - 3000miles = 30points

3000 - 5000miles = 40points

5000miles+ = 50points

Monarch Airlines
Destination Helsinki Fin.
Distance_____ Travel Score 380

Airmiles	Tally	Total
5		
10		
25		
50		
100		
250		
500		
1000		

Virgin Airlines
Destination Fairbanks Alaska 200
Distance_____

Airmiles	Tally	Total
5		
10		
25		
50		
100		
250		
500		
1000		

Aer Lingus
Destination Manila, Phil:
Distance_____ Travel Score 330

Airmiles	Tally	Total
5		
10		
25		
50		
100		
250		
500		
1000		

Easyjet Airlines
Destination Churchill Canada 160
Distance_____

Airmiles	Tally	Total
5		
10		
25		
50		
100		
250		
500		
1000		

British Airways
Destination Suva Fiji
Distance_____ Travel Score 280

Airmiles	Tally	Total
5		
10		
25		
50		
100		
250		
500		
1000		

passport control

If the airline crew have reached their destination they go to 'Passport Control' and have their passports signed and stamped (by the teacher).

The distance is then translated into a travel score that is on-going throughout the year. Their cards are wiped clean, a new destination is chosen and the process begins again. Each crew's flight path is plotted on the map and each half term crews choose one of their destinations as a research topic for homework.

Passport Arrival Confirmation

Destination: _Dublin_

Well Done!!
Arrived at Destination

Miles travelled to destination: 213 x 4

Signed: _Mr McH..._
Date: _14.9.01_

Passport to the World

Refuel

Flight Stop Over For ___ Days!

Lost air miles

Two warning cards can be used.

Refuel
This is when a group is not working at their best. They must improve and have the refuel card withdrawn before the end of the session or they lose air miles.

Flight stop over
This is issued when the group has not worked hard at all. Their airline is grounded for a number of days during which no air miles can be awarded.

Refuel

Try not to get one of these.

This will be given out to your flight crew if they are not working as well as they can. This could mean your crew may lose airmiles if the card is still in your flight pack at the end of the season.

Flight Stop Over

Try not to get one of these.

Your flight crew will be unable to obtain any airmiles for the number of days written on the front of the stop over card.